# Tell Me About It

Anne Montgomery

One is soft.

One is hard.

One is wet.

One is dry.

One is hot.

One is cold.

One is **rough**.

One is smooth.

One is **flat**.

One is round.

One is fast.

One is slow.

One is young.

One is old.

One is big.

One is small.

# Let's Do Science!

How can you describe things like a scientist? Try this!

## What to Get

- 3 things you can hold and look at, such as an apple, a twig, or an eraser
- paper and pencil

# What to Do

1 Make a chart like this one. Write the names of the three things you chose.

| Item | Sight | Touch |
|---|---|---|
| apple | | |
| twig | | |
| eraser | | |

2 Hold each thing, one at a time. Write how it looks under 👁. Write how it feels under ✋.

3 Describe how the things are the same. Describe how they are different.

# Glossary

**flat**—having a wide and smooth surface

**rough**—having a surface that is not smooth

# Index

# Your Turn!

Look at this mug of hot chocolate. Describe it every way you can.

## Consultants

**Sally Creel, Ed.D.**
Curriculum Consultant

**Leann Iacuone, M.A.T., NBCT, ATC**
Riverside Unified School District

**Jill Tobin**
California Teacher of the Year
Semi-Finalist
Burbank Unified School District

**Publishing Credits**

Conni Medina, M.A.Ed., *Managing Editor*
Lee Aucoin, *Creative Director*
Diana Kenney, M.A.Ed., NBCT, *Senior Editor*
Lynette Tanner, *Editor*
Lexa Hoang, *Designer*
Hillary Dunlap, *Photo Editor*
Rachelle Cracchiolo, M.S.Ed., *Publisher*

**Image Credits:** p.23 FoodPhotogr Eising/age fotostock; p.2 iStock; pp.18–19 (illustrations) J.J. Rudisill; all other images from Shutterstock.

**Library of Congress Cataloging-in-Publication Data**

Montgomery, Anne (Anne Diana), author.
Tell me about it / Anne Montgomery.
pages cm
Summary: "It is time to learn how to describe things."—Provided by publisher.
Audience: K to grade 3.
Includes index.
ISBN 978-1-4807-4526-1 (pbk.) —
ISBN 978-1-4807-5135-4 (ebook)
1. Science—Methodology—Juvenile literature.
2. Observation (Scientific method)—Juvenile literature.
3. Readers (Primary) I. Title.
Q175.2.M65 2015
507.2—dc23
2014008625

**Teacher Created Materials**
5301 Oceanus Drive
Huntington Beach, CA 92649-1030
http://www.tcmpub.com

**ISBN 978-1-4807-4526-1**



Printed by: 51497
Printed in: China